EDGE BOOKS™

FULL THROTTLE

CHOPPERS

by
Jeff Savage

Consultant:
Dan Smith
Resource Development Director
The AMA Motorcycle Hall of Fame Museum
Pickerington, Ohio

CAPSTONE PRESS
a capstone imprint

Edge Books are published by Capstone Press,
151 Good Counsel Drive, P.O. Box 669, Mankato, Minnesota 56002.
www.capstonepress.com

Printed in the United States of America in Stevens Point, Wisconsin.
092009
005619WZS10

Books published by Capstone Press are manufactured with paper
containing at least 10 percent post-consumer waste.

Library of Congress Cataloging-in-Publication Data
Savage, Jeff, 1961–
    Choppers / by Jeff Savage.
      p. cm. — (Edge books. Full throttle)
    Summary: "Describes the first choppers, how modern choppers are built, and
lists popular rallies where owners can display their one-of-a-kind creations" —
Provided by publisher.
    Includes bibliographical references and index.
    ISBN 978-1-4296-3939-2 (lib. bdg.)
    1. Choppers (Motorcycles) — Juvenile literature. I. Title.
TL442.7.S28 2010
629.227'5 — dc22   2009022119

Editorial Credits
Carrie Braulick Sheely, editor; Tracy Davies, designer; Jo Miller, media researcher;
    Laura Manthe, production specialist

Photo Credits
Alamy/Andrew Woodley, 21 (top); AP Images/Doug Dreyer, cover, 5; AP Images/
Las Vegas Sun/Ethan Miller, 28; AP Images/Robert E. Klein, 24; Capstone
Studio/Karon Dubke, 17, 19 (both), 21 (bottom), 22 (right), 23; CORBIS/Reuters/
Fred Prouser, 15 (bottom); Getty Images Inc./Car Culture, 9 (top); Getty Images
Inc./Frazer Harrison, 15 (top); Getty Images Inc./Hulton Archive/Columbia
TriStar, 13; Getty Images Inc./Hulton Archive/MacGregor, 9 (bottom); The Image
Works/HIP National Motor Museum, 10; iStockphoto/James Group Studios, 6;
iStockphoto/ODonnell Photograf, 29; Newscom, 7; Newscom/UPI, 27;
Ron Kimball Stock/Ron Kimball, 22 (left), 25

Artistic Effects
Dreamstime/In-finity; Dreamstime/Michaelkovachev; iStockphoto/Michael
Irwin; iStockphoto/Russell Tate; Shutterstock/Els Jooren; Shutterstock/Fedorov
Oleksiy; Shutterstock/jgl247; Shutterstock/Marilyn Volan; Shutterstock/Pocike

Table of Contents

STANDING OUT IN A CROWD

Citizens of Sturgis, South Dakota, hear a distant hum. It's a sound they recognize — the motorcycles are coming. The bikes turn the corner. The hum is a roar now. The booth workers along Main Street get ready to spring into action. They're expecting another huge crowd for the yearly Sturgis Motorcycle Rally.

As the motorcycles slowly rumble down Main Street, more keep coming — thousands of them! Soon there is just one long blur of black tires and seats, leather jackets, and shiny chrome parts.

Most of the bikes are **factory** motorcycles. But a few choppers stand out from the crowd. Many of these bikes have low seats and high handlebars. Long front **forks** make the bikes seem to stretch forever. Colorful paint jobs give the bikes a look all their own. People nearby turn to admire the creative styling of the choppers.

factory — describes a vehicle built at a factory that still has most of its factory-installed parts

With their creative look, choppers rumble down Main Street in style.

fork — the part of a motorcycle that holds the front tire and contains the front suspension system

Fast Fact: During the Sturgis rally, the number of people in South Dakota nearly doubles.

The Sturgis rally is one of the largest motorcycle events in the world. Almost half a million people attend the rally each year. Yet even at large rallies, choppers get a lot of attention. Their gas tanks are often painted bright colors with wild graphics. **Customized** frames and fenders give the choppers a smooth or bold look. Each chopper design shows the personality of its rider. Admiring the artwork on these one-of-a-kind machines is part of the magic of a motorcycle rally.

Many chopper frames are raised at the front.

customized — changed according to the owner's needs and tastes

Arlen Ness

Arlen Ness is known as the "King of Choppers." In the 1960s, Ness built his own choppers in his garage in San Leandro, California. He also painted customers' motorcycles, charging $125 per paint job. At the time, few shops that sold custom parts existed, so Ness made his own parts. Later, Ness began selling his parts. Bikes were Ness' full-time business by 1969, and the business was booming soon afterward.

Today, Ness sells some choppers along with his custom parts. He even sells custom racing suits and gear. Ness' store in Dublin, California, includes a museum where 40 of his favorite motorcycles are on display. Ness was inducted into the American Motorcyclist Association (AMA) Hall of Fame in 1992.

Arlen Ness

The passion for motorcycles stretches to all corners of the world. It all started with German engineer Gottlieb Daimler. In 1885, he mounted a gasoline-powered engine onto a wooden two-wheeled vehicle. Most people consider this to be the first motorcycle. European companies soon began building and selling hundreds of these machines.

In the early 1900s, U.S. manufacturers joined in. In 1901, the Hendee Manufacturing Company began building motorcycles. Now known as the Indian Motorcycle Company, it became one of the world's largest motorcycle manufacturers by 1912.

In 1903, William S. Harley and Arthur Davidson of Milwaukee, Wisconsin, formed the Harley-Davidson Motor Company. Arthur's brothers Walter and William later joined the company. In 1909, Harley-Davidson introduced the V-twin engine that is still popular today.

By the 1920s, Indian, Harley-Davidson, and several European companies were manufacturing thousands of motorcycles. People used their motorcycles for transportation, recreation, and racing.

Daimler's 1885 motorcycle had two small stabilizing wheels at the rear.

Harley-Davidson motorcycles created a name for themselves on the racetrack during the late 1920s and early 1930s.

STRIPPED-DOWN RACE BIKES

Owners started customizing and "chopping" their factory bikes in the early 1930s. In 1934, the American Motorcyclist Association (AMA) organized class-C races. The races featured factory bikes that raced on dirt tracks.

Some class-C racers chopped off unneeded parts to make their bikes lighter. The reduced weight helped riders gain speed quickly. Occasionally these stripped-down bikes were seen on public roads.

The fierce competition of AMA dirt-track racing led racers to "chop" their bikes for better cornering ability and faster acceleration.

More than 20,000 motorcycles were used during World War II (1939–1945). When American soldiers returned home, they found that U.S. manufacturers were building heavier bikes than their war bikes had been. Many of these veterans had been fighter pilots. Craving excitement, they wanted lighter bikes because they were faster. Others preferred the handling ability or the appearance of simpler, lighter bikes.

Whatever the reason, many veterans started customizing their factory bikes. They removed parts that seemed too big or unnecessary. They took off the windshields. They replaced gas tanks, seats, headlights, and mirrors with smaller ones. They cut down, or "bobbed," the rear fender. These stripped-down motorcycles became known as "choppers."

By the late 1940s and early 1950s, choppers began to take on a certain look. The seat was low, and the handlebars were high. The front tire was skinny and tall. The extra height created more ground clearance to help riders travel on rough roads.

Fast Fact: Choppers and hot rods gained popularity around the same time. Like chopper builders, "hot rodders" often chopped off parts to make their cars lighter. They also added custom parts to increase their cars' performance.

GAINING POPULARITY

In the early 1960s, chopper owners went a step further. They removed all the parts from the motorcycle's frame. They then chopped pieces off the frame and welded it back together. Chopping the frame made the bike lower and even lighter.

Chopper popularity reached new heights in 1969 when the movie *Easy Rider* came out. The hit movie told the story of two bikers who rode their choppers from California to Louisiana. One of the choppers had a stars-and-stripes gas tank that looked like the U.S. flag. Ridden by actor Peter Fonda, the "Captain America" chopper caught the attention of motorcycle enthusiasts everywhere.

People who saw *Easy Rider* wanted their own choppers. Many mechanics began building choppers in their garages. Although there were few how-to resources, some builders got help from magazines like *Street Chopper*. Others ordered custom parts from small shops through the mail. Over time, more choppers hit the highways.

Actors Dennis Hopper (left), Peter Fonda (right), and Jack Nicholson (far right) starred in *Easy Rider*.

Fast Fact: In 2009, Peter Fonda celebrated the 40th anniversary of *Easy Rider* by riding a copy of his movie bike.

HITTING THE BIG TIME

Interest in choppers decreased in the 1980s. By this time, some factory bikes had been built to look more like choppers. These bikes included Harley-Davidson's Super Glide and Wide Glide. Many chopper enthusiasts bought the factory bikes instead of building their own choppers.

In the early 2000s, TV helped chopper popularity soar again. The Discovery Channel aired chopper shows *Motorcycle Mania* and *Monster Garage*. These shows starred chopper designer and builder Jesse James, owner of West Coast Choppers.

American Chopper appeared on the Discovery Channel in 2002. This reality show features the Teutul family of Orange County Choppers. Paul Sr. and his two sons have built many famous bikes, such as the Black Widow and the I, Robot Bike.

Today, there are more than 6 million registered motorcycles in the United States. It's hard to guess how many of these are choppers, but they can be seen cruising the streets almost everywhere.

Fast Fact: Celebrities Keanu Reeves, Kid Rock, and Shaquille O'Neal have bought a West Coast Chopper.

Kid Rock's bright yellow chopper got many admiring looks when he took part in a fund-raising ride in 2002.

The I, Robot Bike was built to celebrate the opening of the I, Robot movie in 2004.

Like factory-made motorcycles, choppers have gas-burning engines between two wheels. But most similarities end there. From air filters to rims, almost any part can be customized on a chopper. One of the best things about building a chopper is that there are no rules!

Builders can spend months or even years on their creations. More information on how to build a chopper is available now than ever before. Dozens of books and magazines provide step-by-step building instructions. An almost endless variety of custom parts can be ordered from catalogs and Web sites.

People can also buy chopper kits. These kits come with a frame and other main bike parts. The kits make building a chopper less costly.

For those who don't want to build their own bikes, many professional designers and custom bike shops are available. Bikes built by professionals often cost more than $100,000.

Motorcycle shops usually have lifts and other equipment to make building a chopper easier.

Fast Fact: Most chopper kits cost between $15,000 and $25,000.

FRAMES AND SUSPENSION SYSTEMS

The frame is a motorcycle's support system. The bike's other main parts attach to the frame. The frame also supports the engine. Frames are made of strong metals such as **chromoly** or steel. Some builders start with a factory frame and chop it to a different size and shape. Others make their own frame. Either way, a chopper frame is almost always longer than a factory frame. Chopper frames also usually have a raised front, or neck.

A frame can be built with a hard-tail, soft-tail, or a swing-arm suspension system. A hard-tail design is the oldest type. It has no rear shock absorbers to smooth out the bike's up-and-down movement. Sometimes hard-tails have springs underneath the seat for a little "give" over bumps. But without shock absorbers, hard-tails can be uncomfortable to ride on rough roads and on long trips.

A soft-tail design is common on modern choppers. The soft-tail suspension system looks like a hard-tail system, but two small shock absorbers are hidden underneath the frame. This design provides a much more comfortable ride than the hard-tail system.

The double-sided swing-arm system is less common for choppers than it is for factory bikes. But it provides the most comfortable ride of the three suspension types. This system includes a large shock absorber on each side of the bike. The shock absorbers are mounted between the rear wheel and the frame.

chromoly — a mixture of the metals chromium and molybdenum

Unlike soft-tail designs, the shock absorbers on a swing-arm suspension system are usually visible.

Fast Fact: Chopper foot pegs are often smaller and positioned farther forward than they are on a factory bike. This position allows the rider to lean farther back, allowing for a more comfortable ride.

FORKS AND HANDLEBARS

A long front fork gives a chopper much of its style. Forks on Harley-Davidsons and other factory cruisers average about 3 feet (.9 meter) in length. But chopper forks can stretch 10 feet (3 meters) or more.

Moving the front wheel forward increases the wheelbase, or the distance between the front and rear wheels. A longer wheelbase makes a bike easier to control at higher speeds and while traveling in a straight line. But at slower speeds and on curvy roads, the bike is often harder to control.

A chopper often has high handlebars. The tallest handlebars are known as "apehangers." A rider holding the handlebars so high looks like an ape hanging from a tree.

ENGINES

Chopper owners want their machines to get noticed. A large, growling engine is a good way to do that. Chopper engines come in all sizes. The 120-cubic-inch motor is popular. An engine of this size produces about 110 horsepower.

Most choppers use the V-twin engine design first made famous by Harley-Davidson. V-twins feature two **cylinders** that are set in a "V" shape. V-twins made by S & S Cycle in Viola, Wisconsin, are some of the most popular chopper engines.

20

The angle of the "V" on a V-twin engine varies, but it's usually set at about 45 degrees.

The handlebars on this Captain America copy are raised even more than they were on the movie bike.

cylinder – a hollow chamber in an engine in which fuel burns to create power

Wheel designs are important to most riders. Many modern choppers have tall, thin front wheels and short, wide rear wheels. Some rear wheels are even wider than car tires.

Wheels can be solid or spoke. A solid wheel combines the rim, **spokes**, and hub in one unit. In this design, the spokes are usually fairly wide. A spoke, or wire, wheel has very thin intersecting spokes joined to the rim.

The number of spokes on a wheel varies. There are usually fewer spokes on a solid wheel. Wire wheels can have more than 250 spokes.

solid wheel

spoke wheel

Some people say the gas tank is the heart of a chopper. It sits above the engine in front of the rider. The tank is usually custom-built to fit the bike. It might match the seat or even the rider's helmet. Tanks are usually made of sheet metal, aluminum, or plastic. Most tanks are shaped like a teardrop.

Teardrop-shaped gas tanks give choppers style, but they usually hold less fuel than factory tanks do.

spoke — one of the metal pieces that connects a wheel's rim to the center hub

FINISHING TOUCHES

Chopper owners want all their bike parts to shine, including the metal ones. Choppers usually get their metallic shine from chrome — and lots of it. Chrome parts are plated, or covered with a thin layer of chrome. A chopper can have an almost endless variety of chrome parts. They can include the handlebars, exhaust pipes, brake pedals, and shift levers. The mirrors, kickstands, license plate brackets, and even the frame may also be chrome.

The paint job is often one of the last finishing touches owners add to their bikes. But it's often a feature owners carefully plan. Like everything else on a chopper, the paint job reflects the personality of its owner.

Most chopper owners hire professionals to do the paint work for their bikes.

24

Cost:	usually at least $40,000; can be more than $150,000
Weight:	about 500 pounds (227 kilograms)
Fuel consumption:	about 40 miles (64 kilometers) per gallon
Top speed:	about 120 miles (193 kilometers) per hour
Frame:	usually steel or chromoly in a hard-tail or soft-tail design
Engine type:	usually a V-twin
Engine power:	usually at least 100 horsepower
Transmission:	five-speed or six-speed
Handlebars:	usually set high; many are apehangers.
Forks:	stretched several feet in length
Tires:	often a thin front tire and a wide rear tire

A custom paint job and shiny chrome make this bike a one-of-a-kind machine.

25

RALLY TIME

Once a chopper is built, it's time to show it off. Many owners enjoy attending motorcycle rallies, or gatherings. Rallies are held throughout the world.

Chopper owners and designers can often win awards for their creations at rallies. Competitions may have categories such as comfort, reliability, and of course, creative design.

FAMOUS RALLIES

Laconia Motorcycle Week in New Hampshire is believed to be one of the first-ever rallies. In 1916, a group of motorcyclists at Weirs Beach in Laconia participated in races and hill climbs. In 1923, the event became known as the Loudon Classic. Today, it is a nine-day event held each June.

In 1936, Clarence "Pappy" Hoel formed the Jackpine Gypsies Motorcycle Club in South Dakota. The Black Hills Motor Classic rally was held two years later. Nine riders took part in a short race. It soon became the Sturgis Motorcycle Rally. In 2008, about 400,000 people attended this rally.

Bike Week in Daytona Beach, Florida, is a 10-day event held each March. The rally started in 1937 with a single race on pavement and sand. Now about 500,000 people attend the rally each year.

Laconia Motorcycle Week is one of the biggest rallies of the East Coast.

Dozens of other large motorcycle events are held across the United States. The Oyster Run is held in September in Anacortes, Washington. It is the largest run in the Pacific Northwest.

A Harley-Davidson dealer created the Laughlin River Run in 1983. It is held the last weekend in April on the border between Nevada and Arizona. This rally features a poker run. Riders stop every few miles to collect a playing card, hoping their five cards will form the best poker hand.

The Golden Aspen Rally began in 1986 in Ruidoso, New Mexico. It is held the third weekend in September. The Golden Aspen is one of three rallies sanctioned by the AMA. The others are the Lone Star Rally in Galveston, Texas, and the Americade in Lake George Village, New York.

A chopper attracts attention at the 2005 Laughlin River Run.

No matter where a chopper goes, everyone notices it. Any owner would tell you that there's no motorcycle quite like a chopper. Owners enjoy knowing that their bike is designed specially for them. Just as a chopper's chrome parts show a reflection, the bike itself is a reflection of its owner.

Long front forks on a chopper make it easy to ride on straight sections of road.

chrome (KROHM) — a coating of a metallic substance called chromium; chrome gives objects a shiny appearance.

chromoly (KROH-muh-lee) — a mixture of the two metals chromium and molybdenum

customize (KUHS-tuh-myz) — to change a vehicle according to an owner's needs and tastes

cylinder (SI-luhn-duhr) — a hollow chamber in an engine in which fuel burns to create power

factory (FAK-tuh-ree) — describes a part or vehicle that was built at a factory; a factory motorcycle still has many of its factory-installed parts, such as the frame, fenders, and handlebars.

fork (FORK) — the motorcycle part that holds the front tire and contains the front suspension system

sanction (SANGK-shun) — to officially approve or support

spoke (SPOKE) — one of the metal pieces that connects a wheel's rim to the center hub

suspension system (suh-SPEN-shuhn SISS-tuhm) — a system of springs and shock absorbers that absorbs a vehicle's up-and-down movements

veteran (VE-tuh-run) — a former member of the armed forces

READ MORE

Dayton, Connor. *Choppers.* Motorcycles: Made for Speed! New York: PowerKids Press, 2007.

Doeden, Matt. *Choppers.* Motor Mania. Minneapolis: Lerner, 2008.

Oxlade, Chris. *Motorcycles.* Mighty Machines. North Mankato, Minn.: Smart Apple Media, 2008.

Young, Jeff C. *Motorcycles: the Ins and Outs of Superbikes, Choppers, and Other Motorcycles.* RPM. Mankato, Minn.: Capstone Press, 2010.

INTERNET SITES

FactHound offers a safe, fun way to find Internet sites related to this book. All of the sites on FactHound have been researched by our staff.

Here's all you do:

Visit *www.facthound.com*

FactHound will fetch the best sites for you!

Index